HIPPOS
IN THE WILD

by Jody Sullivan Rake

Reading Consultant:
Barbara J. Fox
Reading Specialist
North Carolina State University

Content Consultant:
Glenn S. Feldhake
World Conservation Union
Hippo Specialist Group

CAPSTONE PRESS
a capstone imprint

Blazers is published by Capstone Press,
151 Good Counsel Drive, P.O. Box 669, Mankato, Minnesota 56002.
www.capstonepress.com

092009
005619WZS10

Library of Congress Cataloging-in-Publication Data
Rake, Jody Sullivan.
    Hippos: in the wild / by Jody Sullivan Rake.
    p. cm. — (Blazers. Killer animals)
    Summary: "Describes Hippopotamuses, their habitat, hunting habits, and relationship
to people" — Provided by publisher.
    Includes bibliographical references and index.
    ISBN 978-1-4296-4010-7 (library binding)
    1. Hippopotamus — Juvenile literature. I. Title.
QL737.U57R35 2010
599.63'5 — dc22   2009027858

Editorial Credits
Mandy Robbins, editor; Kyle Grenz, designer; Svetlana Zhurkin, media researcher;
    Laura Manthe, production specialist

Photo Credits
Corbis/Jeffrey L. Rotman, 24–25
Getty Images/National Geographic/Beverly Joubert, 14–15
Image 100/Wildlife Wonders, 4–5
Minden Pictures/Mitsuaki Iwago, 10–11
Nature Picture Library/Richard Du Toit, 22–23
Peter Arnold/Biosphoto/Gunther Michel, 16–17; Wildlife, 12–13
Shutterstock/Eric Isselée, cover; Erik Stokker, 28–29; Graeme Shannon, 18–19;
    Herbert Kratky, 20–21; Jay Bo, 8; J. Norman Reid, 26–27; Johan Swanepoel, 6–7

TABLE OF CONTENTS

TERRORS WITH TEETH

The calm of an African watering
hole is interrupted by a loud snort.
Two huge heads pop out of the water.
Their giant mouths open wide.

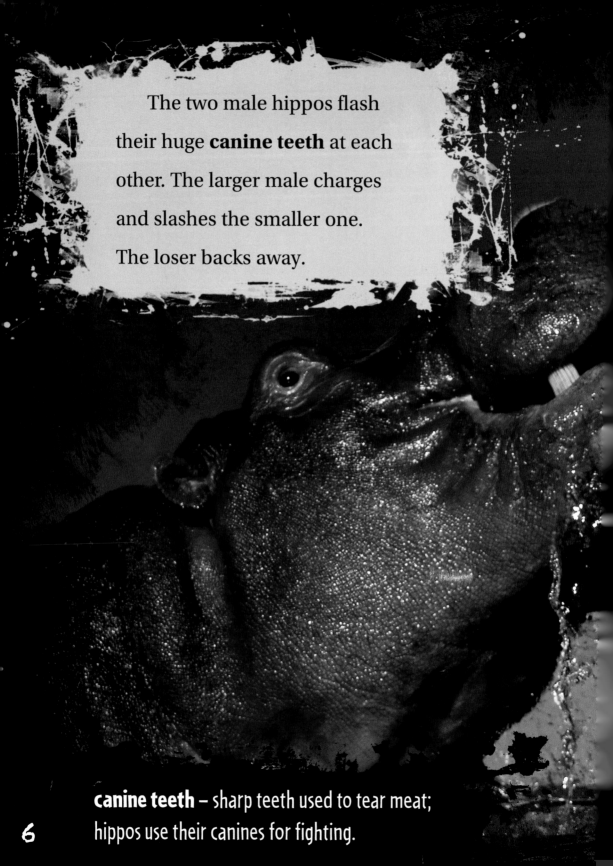

The two male hippos flash their huge **canine teeth** at each other. The larger male charges and slashes the smaller one. The loser backs away.

canine teeth – sharp teeth used to tear meat; hippos use their canines for fighting.

KILLER FACT

Hippos can open their mouths 4 feet (1.2 meters) wide. Their canine teeth grow up to 2 feet (.6 meter) long!

KILLER HIPPOS?

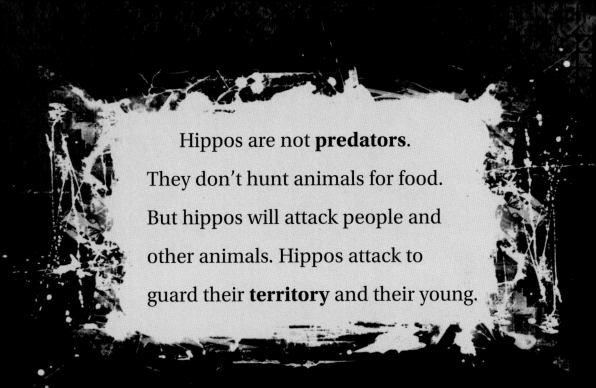

Hippos are not **predators**. They don't hunt animals for food. But hippos will attack people and other animals. Hippos attack to guard their **territory** and their young.

predator – an animal that hunts other animals for food

territory – an area of land that an animal claims as its own to live in

KILLER FACT

Of all land mammals, only elephants and some rhinos are bigger than hippos.

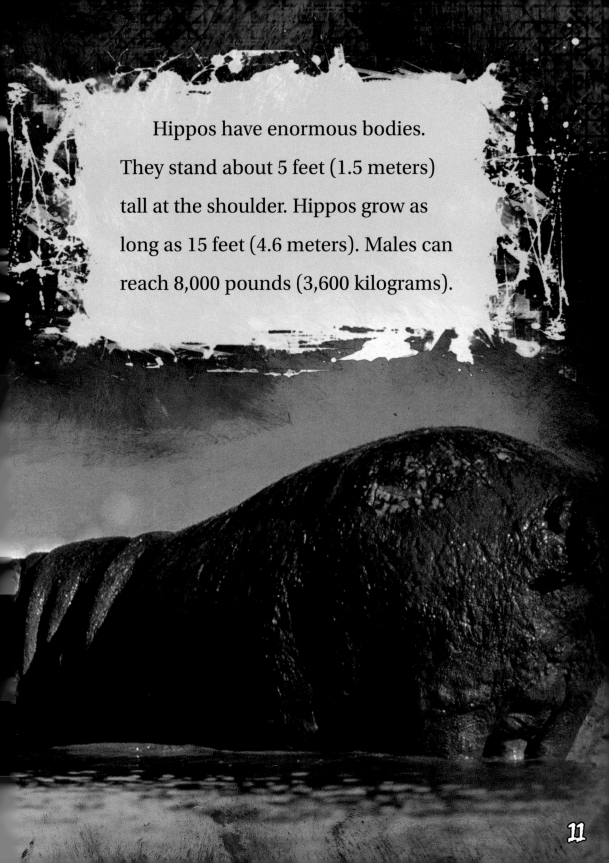

Hippos have enormous bodies. They stand about 5 feet (1.5 meters) tall at the shoulder. Hippos grow as long as 15 feet (4.6 meters). Males can reach 8,000 pounds (3,600 kilograms).

Hippos spend most of their time resting in rivers and **marshes**. But don't be fooled by their heavy, awkward bodies. Hippos can run 19 miles (31 kilometers) per hour.

marsh – an area of wet, low land

KILLER FACT

A hippo's top speed is as fast as the fastest human athletes!

Hippo Diagram

huge jaws

long teeth

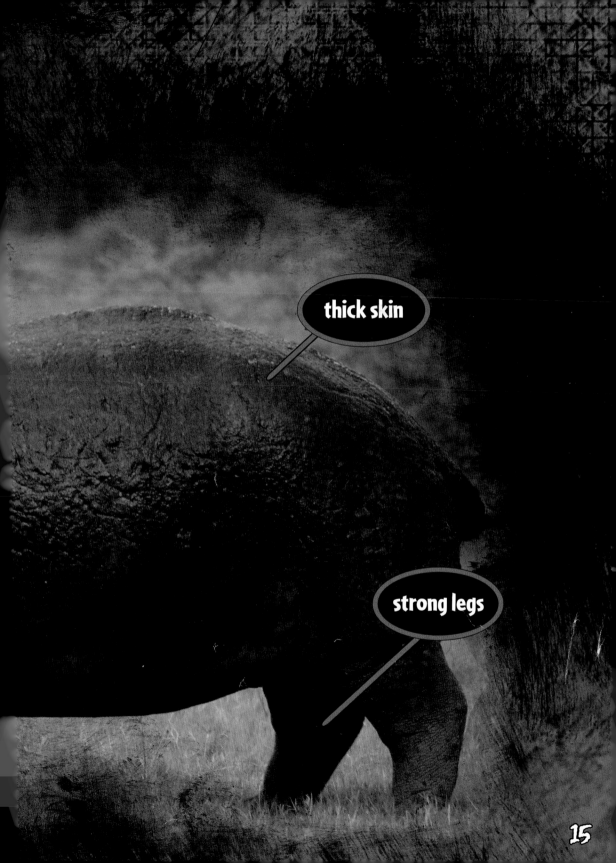

VICIOUS VEGETARIANS

KILLER FACT

Hippos have small appetites. They eat about 88 pounds (40 kilograms) of food per day. That's just 1 percent of their weight.

Hippos are **vegetarians**.
Grasses make up most of their
diet. Hippos usually **graze** at night
when temperatures are cooler.

vegetarian – an animal that only eats plants
graze – to eat grass and other growing plants

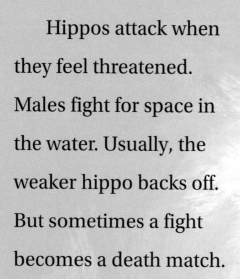

Hippos attack when they feel threatened. Males fight for space in the water. Usually, the weaker hippo backs off. But sometimes a fight becomes a death match.

KILLER FACT

Some male hippos have messy meetings. They turn rear end to rear end and poop on each other!

19

Adult hippos have no predators. But baby hippos are in danger from lions, hyenas, crocodiles, and even male hippos. A mother hippo will fiercely protect her baby from these animals.

KILLER FACT

Hippos kill about
200 people each year.

Hippos are also dangerous to people. Some hippos attack from underwater when boats come too close to them. Other attacks happen at night when hippos come on land to graze.

HIPPOS IN HARM'S WAY

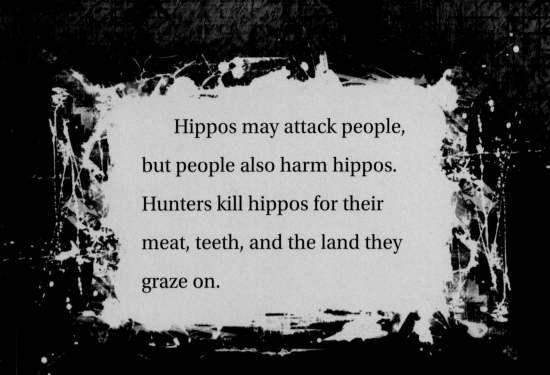

Hippos may attack people, but people also harm hippos. Hunters kill hippos for their meat, teeth, and the land they graze on.

KILLER FACT

People carve hippo teeth into jewelry and decorations.

Hippos once roamed throughout Africa. Now hippos live mostly in **nature preserves**. You can see them in these African parks, but keep your distance!

nature preserve – an area of land set aside for wild animals to live on

Open Wide!

GLOSSARY

canine teeth (KAY-nyn TEETH) — sharp teeth used to tear meat; hippos use their canines for fighting.

graze (GRAYZ) — to eat grass and other growing plants

marsh (MARSH) — an area of wet, low land where grasses grow

nature preserve (NAY-chur pri-ZURV) — an area of land set aside for wild animals to live on

predator (PRED-uh-tur) — an animal that hunts and eats other animals

territory (TER-uh-tor-ee) — an area of land that an animal claims as its own to live in

vegetarian (vej-uh-TAIR-ee-uhn) — an animal that eats only plants or plant products

READ MORE

Clarke, Penny. *Hippos.* Scary Creatures. New York: Franklin Watts, 2009.

Smith, Lucy Sackett. *Hippos: Huge and Hungry.* Mighty Mammals. New York: PowerKids Press, 2010.

Zumbusch, Amelie von. *Hippos.* Safari Animals. New York: PowerKids Press, 2007.

INTERNET SITES

FactHound offers a safe, fun way to find Internet sites related to this book. All of the sites on FactHound have been researched by our staff.

Here's all you do:

Visit *www.facthound.com*

FactHound will fetch the best sites for you!

INDEX